Seasons of Grace

by

Kristen Gowen

Seasons of Grace

A MEMOIR OF LOVE AND OVERCOMING THE UNIMAGINABLE

BY
KRISTEN GOWEN

Copyright © 2025 by Kristen M. Gowen

All rights reserved.

No portion of this book may be reproduced in any form without written permission from the publisher or author, except as permitted by U.S. copyright law.

No part of this publication may be reproduced, distributed, or transmitted in any form or by any means, including photocopying, recording, or other electronic or mechanical methods, without the prior written permission of the publisher, except as permitted by U.S. copyright law. For permission requests, contact Kristen Gowen at chezkriss10@gmail.com.

For privacy reasons, some names, locations, and dates may have been changed.

Book Cover Design by Kristen Gowen

Book Cover Photo by EyeEm from Freepik.com

Illustrations by Freepik.com

First American edition November 2025

October 28, 2025

Hi Baby Girl,

You ready for this?

I love you,

Mama.

Kristen Gowen

Seasons of Grace

Grace in the Fall

My eyes are closed. I breathe in, breath out.

I open my eyes and I register the air is brisk and speaks of fall. Chimney smoke and maybe some snow in the forecast? My favorite time of year. Looking around, I sigh. I just love the light at this time of day. Do they still call it the gloaming after Day Light Savings ends? It's late afternoon and I open the door to the cabin I built a few years ago. It's my place, only a little way from home. The cabin, rustic but more craftsman than 'log,' sits at the top of a mountain rise overlooking a valley. I love that it feels like you're in a treehouse. If you hike down far enough, you'll come to a stream where deer come to drink, maybe a bobcat. There are lots of trees. And lots of squirrels in those trees that taunt Ruby, the resident golden retriever/Australian shepherd.

"Good girl Ru. Go lay down." I open the door wide to let the dog and the air in.

Ruby's an old lady with the most beautiful coat of burnished copper hair and big brown eyes. She jumps onto the overstuffed armchair by the window, the one with the hand-knit afghan, and settles in, smiling at me. Yes. She actually smiles. My dog "smiles." I laugh at her. She knows what today is.

Deep breath. Lemon and wood scents mingle to greet me as I step inside. I have a bouquet of deep red roses with me as I walk through the wood and glass door.

I turn on my entry lamp whose base is a three-figured Hecate statue. The three figures for my three daughters. They are magic. They are ethereal. My lights in a dark world. Warm light glows onto the smiling Buddha statue sitting next to it. I rub his belly and smile.

The entry opens into a large wood beamed great room, but it's not too 'great.' I'd call it 'comfortable.' Big enough for a deep-seated leather sofa and a travertine coffee table and a multicolored rug that has more value as 'cozy' rather than 'valuable.' To the left is another overstuffed chair, but this one rocks. I come from a long line of 'rockers' in my family. At its end is a small, tufted ottoman covered in dark green velvet, perfect to prop your feet on and situated close enough to the tall stone fireplace to warm your feet.

I walk in further and I lay the roses on the kitchen island that sits just off the great room. It's chilly in here, I noticed. I probably should have rethought the large accordion sliding glass doors covering most of the balcony. But that view…

Leaf peepers would weep at this view. Reds, oranges, yellows, browns, greens. I sound like I'm reciting a song by Bruddah Iz. All the colors of the rainbow. So beautiful…

But first. Ooo, it's chilly. Right! Make a fire. Thank God for electric fireplace starters. Next, hmm. Chai tea sounds good. The perfect cup of autumn.

"Alexa, play jazz in the background." Softly, music plays over hidden speakers. I grab my cup of hot, spiced tea and slowly walk around the room, swaying to the music and lightly touching the spines of the books on the floor to ceiling bookshelves. King, Straub, McMahon. Children's books I bought before becoming a mom. *James and the Giant Peach*, *The Stinky Cheese Man*, Christmas books written in French that I can barely read. My dogeared bible. An old journal.

Betwixt and between the books, lie treasures from my travels. There are small paintings I did in college. A shell and a feather. A painted cross a dear friend made me. So many candles. You really can't burn candles in bookshelves. Fire hazard. But they look and smell nice.

Right now, I smell cinnamon. Whether it's from my tea or the candles, I don't know, but it's comforting. Taking a candle from the bookshelf and light it, I set it on the island as I unwrap the roses.

These aren't your average Joe store-bought roses. No. These came from a kind couple who share their bounty with their neighbors. Kind people. I pluck a petal and marvel at just how soft it feels. Bringing it up to my face, I breathe in it's delicate fragrance.

It's almost time.

Today is her 18th birthday. My middle child, my Angel Kiss, has never been one for tangible presents. She's all about the experience. So, this weekend is about us. Just the two of us. I plan, but I don't plan. I'll just see where the weekend leads. Where my girl takes us.

I look out the windows and see that the string of solar lights I hung

3

on the balcony have turned on. Everything bathed in a glow of soft gold. The sky turns a beautiful shade of pink while purple mist wafts around the trees in the valley.

The front door opens, then closes and I feel and smell…fall. "Mama?"

She's here. Karis.

An Autumn Birthday

I turn and watch as my now adult daughter walks through the entryway and I smile. I open my arms wide and gather her in smelling a faint hint of something exotic in her hair. Like petrichor and tropical flowers. She's about my height, just under six feet tall. I grow beautiful babies and she's no exception.

I kiss her cheek and hold her at arm's length to get a good look at her. She smiles.

Her hair is a wild tumble of curls, not quite dark, but not quite blonde either, with wisps of natural blonde highlights framing her face. She has the Merritt deep set eyes from my side of the family. But the color of her eyes reminds me of my maternal grandmother. Cornflower blue. Like my Nana's.

"Happy birthday Angel."

Karis throws her arms around my shoulders. I can feel her smile, and she squeezes me.

"I've missed you Mama," she says.

"I've missed you too. You hungry?"

Karis opens the refrigerator door and takes out a platter of charcuterie I brought for us. "Is this going to spoil our dinner if we eat this?"

"Nah. We can just let the weekend be casual. I really just want to visit. Read a little. Maybe take a walk. Just be. That ok with you?"

"It sounds perfect."

"So," I begin to ask, "what's good?" I learned that's a much better way to start a conversation than 'how are you?' It subconsciously frames your mind to think of good things. I want this time together to be good. Good memories.

"Well," Karis takes a bite of ripe strawberry, "Lark says hi!"

Lark is my 'niece'. Her Mama and I go back a long way. "Aww tell her 'hi' back. I'm sure her mom will be happy to know you saw her."

"Is Aunt Donna doing ok?" Karis questions.

"Yeah, last time I messaged her she was good. Kala, Lark's little sister, is almost Morgan's age. Crazy how our girls are so close in age. But then again, we wouldn't have met otherwise." Karis nods.

Note to self. Reach out to Donna.

"Speaking of sisters what are my two favorite girls up to this weekend? Big Sis and Little Miss," Karis inquires.

I reach across the island and grab a cracker and smear it with cream cheese and jalapeno jelly.

Thoughtfully I look up, "Cam's working. Between that and auditions for this play she's interested in, she's just living her best life in her big girl apartment."

Karis laughs at that. The whole big girl and Big Sis thing with her eldest sister amuses her.

"She say anything about me?"

"She's 23," I reply, somewhat sheepishly. "She's all in her own world right now. She barely has time to reply to my texts. She seems happy though." I glance up.

Karis contemplates. "Hmm. Ok. How's Little Miss?" referring to her youngest sister.

"She has a boyfriend."

Karis chokes a little on the strawberry she's eating, "What?! When did this happen?"

"It's been a couple of months," I reply looking her in the eye. "We met him. Super good guy. Respectful. Kind. It's their first love."

"Uh, what do you mean 'love'? Mom she's 17! How can she possibly know about love at her age."

"Honey, you can't discount someone's first love. You really can't discount love, period." Karis gives me a sideway glance.

"She says to tell you hi," I say.

"She always says 'hi' to me," Karis says. I nod. The bond between these two is strong.

I go to the cabinet and pull down a crystal vase and fill it with water. Karis grabs the roses off the island and puts her face into the bouquet and inhales deeply.

"I love flowers."

I smile at this grown woman standing before me. She is ageless and timeless and yet, I still I can see her in my mind as a baby, a toddler, a precocious little girl. A budding teenager.

This weekend is her birthday present from me, though. Time at the cabin, just the two of us. Where my eldest is practical and prefers money, and my youngest still enjoys unwrapping gifts, this middle child of mine is all about experiences. "Don't get me anything, I just want to go and do and be. Physical presents don't last. Memories do." It's a sentiment I agree with Karis.

I glance out the large picture window and watch the sky darken and marvel at the last of the clouds. Eighteen years. Longer than a decade but shorter than a millennium.

"What would you call an eighteen-year-old?" I ask turning to Karis. "Would you be considered a generation-years-old?"

"Time isn't linear mom. Einstein theory of relativity has proven it."

"Oh, is that so, smarty pants? I suppose he told you that himself."

Karis just smiles.

I reach over to grab a bottle of wine I had opened earlier. I was letting it breathe. Like me. In and out. I grab my favorite wine glass – a gift from my daughters – and pour myself a healthy measure.

"Walk with me, talk with me," I say to Karis as I head toward the balcony door.

Standing at the wrought iron railing, I pull out a pack of cigarettes. I can hear the collective disgust from here, Dear Reader, so consider yourself acknowledged.

"You know those will kill you." My judge and jury have spoken.

"Don't ever try it. Promise me." I flick the lighter and light the tip of my cigarette, breathing in the smoke.

Exhale. Pause. "I've been in therapy," I say.

"You have? Mom, that's so good! Mental health is important. Just as important as your physical health," she says giving me the side eye as she points at the cigarette in my hand.

"Yes 'Mom' I know. I've told you girls about how important your mental health is since you were little." I ignore the cigarette dig. "I guess it's just time that I walk the walk and not just talk the talk."

Karis looks at me. She holds out her hand, and I take it. Turning we watch the trees in the valley sway in the breeze and listen to their hushing sound.

"I'm glad you're here, Baby. I hope you're having a good birthday."

"I am Mama."

"Yeah, I'm just grateful for the times that we can do this." I smile over to my beautiful second born.

"We can do this anytime you want," she says returning my smile. I squeeze her hand, and she squeezes mine back.

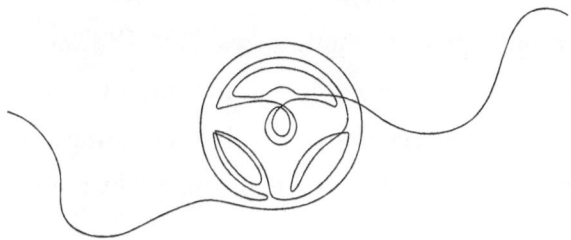

My Randy: Scene One

The first time I met my therapist, Randy, I was dealing with a lot of things. Anxiety, depression, a feeling of dread that I couldn't shake no matter how hard I tried. I wasn't ok. I needed that therapy time. My time, not anyone else's. And I desperately wanted it to work for me.

Randy opens the heavy wood office door for me and calls me in. He looks younger than me and is way taller. I'm 5'11". He probably had at least six inches on me. Funny, he isn't imposing or intimidating. Just a quiet presence probably borne of years of sessions with people like me, and classroom time at the college where he was a full-time professor. Thankfully he only took clients on Fridays, his only day off, and it just worked out that Friday mornings worked great for me.

I started calling him My Randy because it sounded pretentious to me when I would talk to my family about what new skill or takeaway I received from him. Instead of "my therapist says," I'd say "Well My Randy told me…" And that's how he became known as My Randy.

I didn't know his full name when we first met. I didn't learn it until nearly a year after I started meeting with him. That's the honest truth. I didn't want to know. I thought it would keep things in perspective and separated from my 'real life.' This was my 'therapy life.' When I walked in his office, in my mind we were two players performing a one act scene in a black box theater, and for the next 55 minutes, I would be "Kristen" (played by me.) And Randy would play the part of "My Randy."

Alright everybody. Places. Break a leg.

"I'd like to start off by just going over some ground rules with you." My Randy said. "First, this is your time. If you want to talk, we'll talk about whatever is on your mind. If you want to sleep on the couch for your 55 minutes, that's fine too. Just know this is a safe space."

I look around the large room and notice dolls in the corners and a couple of fidget toys on the side table next to me. Large plate glass windows overlook the city. We're high enough off the ground to not feel exposed. It feels more like we're in a treehouse, minus the trees. I grab a pillow from the couch and instinctively cover my stomach, protecting my internal organs from attack. Not because I think Randy would hurt me, but being vulnerable has put me in places where I have been hurt in the past. Randy notices me holding the pillow but doesn't say anything.

Instead, he points at some of the colorful charts and toys strewn around the room.

He explains, "This office actually belongs to one of my colleagues who counsels children. Since I teach counseling at the college, I don't have a permanent office here. It's kind of a nice space though, I like it." He shrugs.

I nod. And wait.

"Next thing I'll tell you is that I don't answer questions."

"So, everything I say needs to be something other than a question," I say. (That's a statement, not a question, I think to myself. I'm off to a good start).

"Correct. I want you to figure things out on your own. Don't ask me how to do things because automatically giving you the answers won't help you. You need to come up with those answers. That way you take ownership of what you figure out." Randy continues, "Now, I will guide you toward discovering things about yourself. Along the way, I can give you tools to use that might be helpful, maybe recommend books that can help get you from point A to B."

Ok. Fair enough. My time. No questions. Homework. Got it.

"Let's just see how it goes," he says.

Apparently, Randy has more to say, "When we start a session, I don't like to ask 'how are you?' You may be in a terrible place but not ready to discuss or dig into that yet. I don't want to push the narrative. So I'll just say, 'What would you like to talk about today?'"

Fair enough. I'm a rule follower. I can do this.

For the next 55 minutes I give him the general overview about me, like you might give in a job interview. Touch on family, marriage, job. Then I start to toe the therapy waters and explain I'm not sleeping well, problems with feeling overwhelmed by life, life has no color. I've recognized I shrink back into myself so I can avoid conflict, vulnerability, issues I'd rather avoid than deal with straight on. I tell My Randy that I've been diagnosed with depression. I'm currently on medications for that, but something new has cropped up. Anxiety. It's overwhelming, dark, and I worry about everything. My hands shake a little. Randy takes notice but doesn't call attention to it. I set the pillow down beside me that I was holding, still close but not covering me. I stroke it like a cat to comfort myself. I feel vulnerable but I'm going to trust this is a safe place. First step of 'faith' in therapy, I suppose.

"We're getting close to the end of our time today," Randy says. "Before you leave, I want ask you to do an exercise for me. You can do it in the car on the way home.

"Turn your radio off so you're not distracted. First I want you to just sit there for a minute. Close your eyes. Pay attention to how your body feels. Is it tense? Relax your shoulders. Relax your jaw. Breathe. Next turn on the car and grab the steering wheel. Is the steering wheel hard or is it soft? Smooth or bumpy? Next, what do you hear? Is it the heater turning on and blowing or the road noise as cars drive on the street? What do you smell, is it your coffee sitting next to you? Old French fries your kids ate in the back seat earlier?

"Now I want you to drive home. Pay attention to what you see. Pay attention to colors or patterns. Look at the sky. Safely!" My Randy reminds me. "Keep your eyes on the road. I don't want a phone-call next week saying you had to reschedule because you're in the hospital. I'll see you next Friday."

I smile and tell him thank you.

End scene.

But I'm not done with therapy today. I still have to 'rehearse' this scene if I'm going to get better at my part in this scenario. I get in the car. I'm going to take this seriously. I need help. This will help. Please God let this help. Even just a little bit.

I spend a moment, just paying attention. I recall Randy's guidance. The steering wheel is hard and cold. I squeeze it. I smell the coffee I brought with me and picking it up, take a drink. It's a little colder than I like, but that's ok. I start the car.

On the drive I make notes of colors - yellow stripe in the road. Purple in the graffiti on that business' wall that I never noticed. But I noticed it today. Wonder how long that's been there? I stop at a stop light. The light is so vivid red. Is this what happens when you are present in the moment and just pay attention? Does everything appear to be more real? Is this just my first lesson in how to be present again in my own life?

By the time I get home I'm surprisingly relaxed. The anxiety and depression are still there, but now, I feel like I can breathe. I'll take that as a first therapy session win.

I imagine an small audience clapping. 'Well done! Encore!' Mentally, I take a bow.

Kristen Gowen

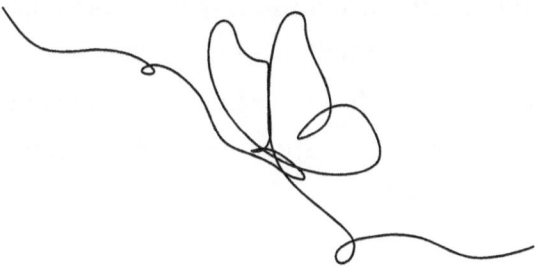

Grace in the Beginning

Want to hear something funny? Getting pregnant with Karis started as a dare. I swear to God. Here I was, nearly 40 years-old with a four-year-old daughter and wondering if I could *possibly* have another baby at this age. Crazy right? Who in their ever-loving mind thinks, 'Hey, I want to see if I can get pregnant again, defying all the odds?' This girl apparently.

The joke was on me. Within two months of trying, I got pregnant. We're talking giddily, happily, and somewhat arrogantly saying, 'look at us!' I was a 'mature' mom when I had my oldest daughter, Cameron, at 35. This time, I was pushing the limits.

To say we were in a good place at the time is an understatement. We were in a place where we could comfortably add to our family. That was a huge blessing and relief. I remember just giggling that I was in fact pregnant and felt so incredibly happy. My pregnancy with Cameron had been difficult. Medically, I had some leg swelling that eventually put me on restricted work and early maternity leave, but I was also commuting throughout my pregnancy by driving to my job two hours away. I worked in corporate America and the expected workload required long hours and was stressful.

I can honestly say this second time around was a perfect pregnancy. Now I was working from home for myself and I was involved in my daughter's life and my church. My life was vibrant and fulfilling. I remember my dad and I had signed up at our church to help with a basketball camp the church sponsored. I was probably about four months along and feeling great – past the overwhelmingly tired phase. Feeling good enough to shoot hoops and practice with the kids at the camp, but not too far along that my growing belly held me back. We were just about done with a particular session when I first felt the baby kick. Just a flutter, like butterflies, but I remember being so excited and telling my dad, "Guess someone's excited to play basketball someday." I remember the look on his face – part wonder and part excitement. If how he loved my eldest daughter, who coincidentally was named after him, was an indication, this grand-baby was going to be loved beyond measure. I'm semi-sure my folks had resigned themselves to the fact that they'd only have one grandchild. Adding a second one was something – and someone – we all eagerly anticipated.

When I was pregnant with my first born, we opted not to know the gender. I really wanted that feeling of getting the biggest surprise. I love surprises! Cameron Elizabeth was perfect, obviously (says the proud mom). But my heart already knew I was carrying a girl. Ok, there was that one dream that I was carrying a blonde, blue-eyed puppy, but I digress.

This time, with our second pregnancy, we opted to find out the gender. Because of my advanced age with all my pregnancies, it was recommended that I have an amniocentesis. Honestly, *whispers* getting an amnio wasn't a big deal for me. You have about a 20-minute ultrasound where you get to see your baby move and kick around while the doctor counts all the fingers and toes and points out what grey blob is a leg and what is a nose. Yes, there's a big needle involved, but afterward you get to go to lunch and lay around for the rest of the day. Not a bad day for a pregnant lady.

Cameron was the reason we decided to find out the gender that day. Plus, I really wanted to be prepared depending on whether it was a boy or a girl. When Baby Cameron was born and we announced, "It's a GIRL!" my parents went out and bought a few dozen outfits. "Few" may be a conservative number looking back – but everything was all pink and/or frilly. So, our thinking was that confirming the sex of the baby would offset a major shopping spree.

In all honesty, I also wanted to decorate an all-boy or all-girl nursery. We're talking full blown, pink or blue, not something neutral in the least. There would be no question if we were going to be having a boy or a girl this time. Cameron was so excited to be a big sister, and she really wanted to know if it was a brother or sister she'd have as her forever best friend. So, we asked the doctor to tell us. "It's a GIRL!"

We surprised Cameron with a gift bag containing two matching shirts that we bought from the hospital gift store. One shirt for her that said, "I'm the big sister" and one shirt that was so tiny that said "I'm the little sister." That GirlChild of mine, our Cameron, was so happy to know she was having a baby sister! And the plans she already had in her little four-year-old mind had already solidified.

They would be best friends. They'd share a room when the baby was old enough to have a matching twin bed. And her favorite color would definitely be pink. Because it was, of course, her big sister's favorite color as well.

I was fortunate to work from home as a freelance graphic designer and had an awesome boss (me), and my dad was semi-retired, so the two of us repainted and redecorated the two kids bedrooms at our leisure. Cameron's bedroom was this gorgeous ballet slipper pink. The nursery was a soothing sage green. We even had a twin bed in the nursery along with the crib in anticipation of the girls sharing a room in the future. I was able to find matching shabby chic quilts covered in pink and green roses that went perfectly with the wall colors we had chosen.

It was so girly. Lots of antiques, pastel tchotchkes, and refinished furniture. Pink patchwork and wire butterflies on the wall. My dad had even built matching headboards for the girls using the jenny Lind crib they had at their house when Cameron was a baby. And, in the nursery window, was a wood and ribbon banner with the letters that spelled 'ANGEL.' It was originally in Cameron's old baby nursery, and I had saved it. I painted the letters with that same ballet pink Cameron had chosen for her room.

We couldn't keep calling the baby "Peanut," which is what we called all our babies before they had names. So, we started our baby name list. Most of the names we considered were family names, but this time we both had a real heart reaction to the name "Karis." Karis is Greek for "grace." We loved how beautiful and unique it was. We then made the unconventional decision to let Cameron pick out her baby sister's middle name so she would feel more involved with the pregnancy and with Karis. "I think Juliana is the most beautiful name in the world!" she told us. We have no idea where that came from, but we didn't question it. It seemed perfect. So that's how Karis Juliana got her name.

For a number of years, I had already been very involved with my church, in particular a women's bible study made up mostly of women around my age and a few a bit older. My pregnancy was a surprise to all my friends, and they were anticipating Karis's arrival maybe just as much as we were. I think, in a way, it was a novelty because most of my friends' children were way older and being around someone pregnant at my age was something out of the ordinary and something we could all be excited about.

I had built-in aunties and uncles and babysitters and extra grandparents lined up in anticipation of this little bundle of joy. A big church-wide baby shower celebration was scheduled for 11/11/07. Eleven eleven is an angel number, I've read. A perfect day. I couldn't wait! Plenty of time before my daughter was to be born. Her anticipated birthday was to be Christmas Day. She was going to be the most precious gift.

Grace: at the Hospital

Let me be honest. My pregnancy with Karis was a joy. I felt great, had great doctor visits. My favorite visits were when I could see Karis on sonograms. I got lots of those, too, because of my high-risk status. My ultrasound technician was the sweetest lady. She raised miniature donkeys in her spare time and had pictures on her computer. She shared with me how she enjoyed knitting. We'd have these great conversations while she scanned and measured Karis and took pictures for me to bring home and show to my family and friends.

Karis was my little 'attached buddy.' We'd dance in the living room to *Into the Mystic*, sang in the car (ok, I was doing all the work, she just came along for the ride). We played with Big Sis who was easing out of her Wizard of Oz phase and heading straight into her Hannah Montana era. Cameron turned five in September and here it was just the first week in November. My favorite season. Fall.

I remember we had bought a rocker recliner in anticipation of late nights nursing and wanting a place to rest, rock, and relax with the baby. My ex was great with our babies. He had a 'magic' shirt, soft and warm, that he cuddled our babies against. When he was home on the weekends, he took over, stating, "weekends are 'my' time with 'my girls.'"

I think it was a Tuesday when I started experiencing some Braxton Hicks contractions that continued off and on. I tried getting comfortable in the new recliner, but the uncomfortableness kept up.

My parents had just returned from a two-week long cruise to Hawaii and they had been anxious that somehow this baby would get here before they returned. They had been home two days when I called my mom and told her I just wasn't feeling 100%. She offered to pick me up and let me hang out with her for a while.

A little Hawaiian baby dress lay on their table in the kitchen when I arrived at their home. All us girls got Hawaiian dresses from their travels, but this was just beautiful. A tiny dress that was dark robin's egg blue and covered with flowers. My dad grew up in Hawaii, so I knew he probably picked this out for his little mo'opuna (granddaughter).

As the morning progressed, I really had this gut feeling that I needed to get checked out by a doctor. If anything, I might need some sort of medication to stop the contractions, or maybe, just maybe, I might need to have this baby early. I prayed 33 weeks would have allowed her to develop enough in case I was indeed in labor.

I jumped in my parent's shower and soaped up my belly telling Karis she needed to stay in my belly just a little while longer because we had a baby shower that coming Sunday. I came out of the bathroom to find my mom in her dressing area putting on earrings of all things.

"Mama, we're just going to get me checked out, you don't need to get fancy with jewelry."

"I may be meeting my newest granddaughter today," she said. "I want to look pretty for her."

We drove the 45 minutes it would take to get to the hospital ER. I got in a wheelchair and was wheeled into check-in. I explained to the nurse that I wasn't ready to have this baby just yet and probably just need some medication, so she stays "cooking" a little longer. "She's not due until Christmas. And my baby shower is in four days!" I exclaimed.

So many people had made plans, RSVP-ed. It was going to be the most epic baby shower ever.

"Oh, I'm sure it's just something like that," the nurse said. "Let's get you into triage and on a monitor and see what's up."

I lay on the gurney in triage while my mom – in her earrings – waited for me just outside in the waiting room. It's not a fancy place, triage. Just a way-station to where they really want to take you. It's mostly gray. Or at least I remember it as gray. They really should rethink that color.

"I'm going to hook you and the baby to a heart monitor. This is going to be a little cold," the nurse said as she squirts the gel on my stomach for the fetal doplar. "It's ok, I've had lots of scans being an older mom. I love being able to see her."

"Oh, we're just trying to find where she is so we can put this monitor on to keep an eye on her heart rate," the nurse says as she holds up the elastic belt with a blue disk in the middle. Rubbing the wand over my belly, she starts slowly scanning for Karis. "She must be hiding in there," the nurse tells me with a smile. "I feel like I'm having to chase her down. I can hear her heart faintly; I'm just having trouble finding a good spot where it's strong so I can hook your monitor up."

I'm not worried. We've been dancing the last few days until my contractions started. Karis is probably tired. "I'm going to call your doctor and let her take a look," the nurse says and pats my leg. I'm lying on this grey gurney in this grey room. I may have been alone. I honestly can't recall. I stare at the fetal heart monitor still not hooked up to me, but rub my belly and tell Karis to hang on a bit longer. The doctor's coming and she'll know what to do.

My doctor is unfairly beautiful. This is no lie. She has long blonde hair and a beautiful face. She made me feel instantly at ease and cared for from the first time we met. I felt that same way when she rounded the corner in the ER triage and said, "Hey Kristen, ok, let's see what's going on here."

With her, dragging behind, is a ultrasound machine. I knew she'd come in meaning business and I settled down to let her do her thing.

Holding the bottle of gel she says, "This is going to be a little cold."

This is becoming a theme, I think nervously in my head. Several seconds, minutes, pass. It could have been almost instantly. I just remember the doctor taking my hand.

Randy Session: Trust

"Good morning," I say to My Randy.

"Good morning, what would you like to talk about today?"

I sit on the couch facing him. I leave the pillow where it is this time.

"Same stuff. Just dealing with a lot and it's overwhelming me. I ruminate for hours, search the Internet for answers."

"Don't believe everything you read on the Internet," he says. "Doom-scrolling will just make things feel worse."

"I know, but I feel I've got to plan for every possible situation. I lay awake at night filled with anxiety wondering 'what if?'"

"Hold on," Randy says standing, "switch places with me."

I get up and sit in the chair he just occupied earlier and face the couch. He takes my place.

"Thanks, go on. You were saying?"

"I was saying I feel like I need to plan every contingency, so I'm prepared when something bad hap…."

At that moment Randy grabs the pillow off the sofa and throws it at my head.

I'm quick, I pluck the pillow out of the air before it can hit me in the face. I'm a little stunned. Then I kind of chuckle and look at him. I toss him the pillow back.

"Uh. Like I was saying…"

"Hold on," Randy stops me. "What just happened?"

"Um, you threw that pillow at me."

"And then what happened."

"I caught it and threw it back to you."

"Uh huh. And were you expecting me to do that?"

"No."

"But it happened. And you caught it. You dealt with the unknown obstacle, and you reacted. You didn't panic. You just dealt with the problem and threw it back to me." Randy continued, "Now if I had warned you before we switched places and said, 'Kristen, at some point during our time I'm going to throw a pillow at your head,' what would you do?"

"I'd probably be worrying about when you were going to throw that pillow at me instead of what I was talking about or doing," I said.

"Right. In that moment, you trusted yourself to catch the pillow. You've played basketball. You've probably made thousands of catches. I threw a pillow to show you that you can handle obstacles thrown at you and not be afraid."

Huh. I nod. I can catch problems thrown at me, deal with them, throw it back. Not be concerned if it will happen, just confident that I can face whatever comes my way and deal with it.

Granted, life isn't going to just throw pillows at you. Some things may be completely out of your control. But you can trust yourself to handle these things without being afraid.

I've faced hard things before. Really hard things. Unfathomable things. But I survived every one of them. One hundred percent of them. I just lost trust in myself somewhere along the way. I want to face my fears and trust I can overcome whatever happens.

Grace in the Winter

It's breezy on the pier overlooking blue water. Lazy clouds drift by quietly surveying me, like I'm about to do something worth noting. I take a bite of a mango from trees that grows wild on the island. Juice runs down my chin and it tastes like everything that is good in this world. This is my happy place. This spot. I've even painted it on a 4'x4' canvas just so I can always remember how I felt when I first sat here eating my first ever mango. Winter is hard and spending it in this peaceful place is a dream.

Here you can snorkel or scuba dive and experience every underwater wonder you could imagine. It's late afternoon. Everyone had gone inside the beach house for a late nap before going out for a night dive.

I hear Karis before I see her.

"Hey, you gonna share some of that with me?"

"It would be a really Mean Mom move to not let you have a bite. You get your love of mangoes honestly. I think I craved them daily when I was pregnant with you."

"Huh, what did you crave with my sisters?"

"Cameron, definitely sushi and watermelon. Morgan? Margaritas."

I hear her laughter over the wind. "Margaritas? Really?"

"So much so, that your Papa brought me a four-pack of margaritas after Morgan was born. I promise, I only drank one in the hospital." I smile at the memories.

Karis crouches next to me and looks out at the horizon as she takes a bite of the mango. Squinting her eyes she asks, "Wanna take a walk with me and watch the sun set?"

She stands and reaches for my hand and smiles, dimples she gets honest, on full display. The ocean breeze lifts her curls and partially covers her face. She got those curls from me. Genetics are a crazy thing and I'd love to take all the credit for this beautiful creature's attributes. But she is purely Karis. I'm just a grateful spectator who can see her in my mind's eye anytime I want. And I'm so grateful I can. She's just old enough to be considered a teenager but will forever be my baby.

I take her hand, soft like a rose petal, and she pulls me up.

"Ugh," I grunt. "Getting old is not for the faint of heart."

"Age is a privilege denied to many."

I look at her. Wise beyond her years.

"Where did you hear that?"

"Oh, I don't know," she replies. "It's just some quote I heard. Come on. Before the sun sets."

We don't talk for a while as we walk slowly in that sweet spot between sand and the waves washing in. I pull my cover-up around me. It still winter in paradise and as the sun starts to set, it gets chillier. Karis picks up a piece of driftwood and kneels in the sand. Lazily she writes her name, and when she finishes, dots the "I" with the stick, leaving it stuck in the sand. Sunset is one of those magical times where time seems to speed up and almost race to the horizon. I notice the stick has become a makeshift sundial with its shadow growing longer as the sun dips further toward the ocean.

"Watch this mama," Karis says.

I look up from the sundial and marvel as the blaze of brilliant pink into purples that have exploded above our heads.

"My God, that's beautiful."

Karis turns and smiles at me. "I thought you'd like it."

"Do you ever wonder what's beyond the sunset?" I ask.

I may be getting a little philosophical, more than most teenagers can appreciate but Karis is an old soul. She doesn't like small talk. She would rather think the big thoughts and really listen to what a person's heart is saying.

Karis answers. "Stars."

So much for a philosophical talk. That makes me smile. Everything about this time makes me smile.

"It's gonna get dark soon, Angel, we should think about heading back to the house. Make sure we pick up any bottle caps in the 'yard.'"

It doesn't suck that our 'yard' here is an oceanfront white sand beach, covered with coconut trees and every tropical flower you can imagine, just growing wild.

"Mama, can we stay just a little longer and watch the stars?"

"But it's gonna get dark soon. The 'rawrs' might come out and getcha!" I'm trying to sound funny but to me I sound off.

Karis laughs. I love when she laughs. But I feel more than see the darkness coming.

"Don't worry Mom. I'm here."

She's not afraid of the dark. She faces it head on. I wish I was brave like her.

Karis looks up and the heavens explode above us. Orion's Belt. Big Dipper. Little Dipper. The Milky Way is showing off. Unsure how we can see all of this or how to take it all in. It's overwhelming. A little frightening to think you're just a tiny speck in this vast universe and yet, still feel as if a universe lives inside of you.

"Full disclosure," I say, "I sometimes am afraid of the dark. Even after all this time."

"I'm not afraid Mom."

"Never?"

"Nope."

"Mama," Karis says. "Tell me about the night I was born."

And all I see and feel is darkness.

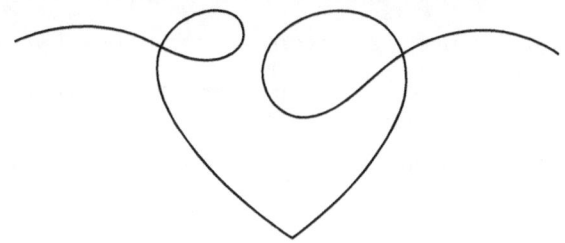

Grace in Darkness

"Oh honey, Her heart's not beating anymore. I'm so sorry. She's gone."

What? What did the doctor just say?

Someone is screaming. I feel it more than I hear it. But my hair stands up on my neck and arms. It's a guttural wail. If you've ever heard the sound, it's something that sticks *with* you and *to* you. It's a dark ripping pain. A primal, wordless scream that comes from the deepest depth a person can fathom. It's hope died. It's panic and fear and despair. I don't know how better to describe it, which is odd because it's me. That scream came from me.

"Her heart was beating!" I exclaim. "The nurse could hear it. I don't understand." I blurt out, tears streaming down my face.

"It was *your* heart she heard. Not Karis's. Karis's heart has stopped. She died." Bless her, she was trying so hard to explain the unexplainable to me.

I'm sobbing. My doctor is looking a me and to the screen in shock. I don't know what to do but grab her and hug her and tell her, "I'm so sorry. I'm so sorry you had to be the one to tell me." When you're trying to make sense of something, you do and say crazy things, I guess. My gut reaction was to comfort her. I guess I wanted to be the comfort for someone – anyone – like I needed right then.

"Honey, you're the one I should be comforting. You did nothing wrong. You have nothing to apologize for."

"Can my mom come back here please?" I ask.

And that's where I blank out for a while. I know my mom came into triage and just hugged and cried with me. She called my dad and asked him to pick up Cameron from school. It's Wednesday, church night. All our church family and friends would be at church. I called the one friend whose phone number I had memorized (and could recall) since this was the time before I had contacts in my cell phone. Thank God she answered. She was already up at the church. I told her through tears my Karis was gone, I'm at the hospital, I have to deliver her.

It's four days before my baby shower. Except instead of a baby shower, I would plan a memorial. My beautiful Karis Juliana had died in utero at 33 weeks. It was November 7, 2007.

You know how gossip spreads? Well tragic news spreads even faster in a church that loves you. I don't mean that in a bad way at all. I'm just saying that church people, especially the Methodist church I belonged to, when tragedy struck, it was all hands on deck.

I need to preface the next bit because it comes in sparks and jumbles, just like any grief-laden tragedy. But I'll try to be mindful of the timeline.

I remember knowing Cameron would be ok. A friend offered to bring her home with her and let her spend the night since we were undoubtedly staying at least a night at the hospital. I remember my Daddy coming in and kissing me with tears in his eyes and my mom clinging to him. My understanding is that just about everyone who had come to church for supper that Wednesday caravaned to the hospital and waited in the waiting room. They didn't all come in my room. But they were praying for all of us. I was in a delivery room, the lights dim except certain lights over the white board and where the bassinet sat. I had already changed into a gown and had an epidural put in. I know this because I was no longer in physical pain.

Then the sister-girlfriends came in. That's what I called them back then. They were my extended chosen family. I hadn't been at the church, or should I say, fully involved, but for a few years. But they loved and cared for me fiercely. I felt it. And they came in to love me, to be with me, to pray for me, before I delivered Karis. They even told me a story and made me laugh through tears. I think it was something about one of my friends getting into an almost physical altercation with someone in the waiting room? I honestly can't be certain, but that feels right. I remember one of the others telling this friend, "I'll walk you to your car. That guy won't mess with you. Don't worry."

And someone so kind, said even in the midst of this tragedy, I glowed. I really felt God close then, surrounding me. It was a warm, peaceful feeling and I felt only love. I'm not sure how, but that's what I felt. You can tell me it was the medication they had me on if you want. I don't care. When you're in that place of grief, you'll take anything to alleviate the suffering, I'm sure. I had God.

Flash forward to Karis's delivery. Time was quiet. It didn't tick tock. It just silently moved through the room. I remember being alone? I say that with a question because to be honest, I only felt myself, my doctor, and maybe one nurse in the room. I recently asked my Mom, who has been with me through all my deliveries, if she was there.

"Of course I was, Baby. But I can understand why you felt alone. You were solely focused on bringing Karis into the world. Everything else didn't matter."

I could still fool myself into thinking somehow, some way, Karis would prove them wrong with all their scans and test and come out crying and alive. I held onto the nurse telling me in triage "I hear her heartbeat faintly," only to be told it was my heartbeat they heard. Doctors are wrong sometimes. They're not God. God will see His mistake, see Karis worthy of life. He'll save her. I was so hopeful. Maybe that's why I glowed. I just wanted to hang onto her life force and I wanted to believe that she shined through me, against the odds, and say, "See? God prevails!"

The lights were turned low. I remember my unfairly beautiful doctor speaking softly to the nurse. There was a halo of light above her and shining down where Karis would arrive. My eldest, Cameron Elizabeth, was 8 lbs 13 oz at birth. I spent MANY hours pushing to deliver that precious child and was so relieved when she arrived screaming at the top of her lungs. Karis, in comparison, came in a couple of pushes, silently drifting into this world. So quiet. No sound. I only saw her hand before the doctor handed her to the nurse who was waiting for her. The doctor cut the cord and severed the only physical link that connected us.

"Can I donate her organs? Her skin? Anything to make her life make sense and help others?"

"No," I was told. "She died too long ago and nothing is viable or salvageable. I wish we could."

Karis Juliana was born perfect and weighed 3 lbs. 11 oz. and was 17.5" long.

The nurse took Karis away to clean her as best as possible. Friends and family drifted through. I don't remember details. During one of those rotations of people, the nurse brought Karis in, wrapped in a hospital blanket and wearing a soft, ballet pink dress with little pink flowers on it. She had a little hat that matched, covering her head and brow. Resting on her chest was a hand-sewn heart made of the same fabric, framed in delicate white lace. In her hand, they had placed a tiny pearl rosary.

I don't think it registered to me others were in the room. The lights were still dim. I don't think I could move my legs after the epidural just yet. But I marveled at my beautiful daughter. The nurse asked everyone to give us some privacy. She said I could spend some time with Karis if I wanted. I don't think I responded, I just picked her up. She was warm. Was she still warm from delivery or from the heating pad they had placed beneath her while they dressed her, I don't know. I just remember her being warm. I did like all parents do. I lifted her hat and saw she was nearly bald and blond just like her big sis. Her eyes were closed but I knew, I just knew they were cornflower blue. Karis had the most beautiful long fingers, like a piano player. And long legs that would be strong like a ballerina or a basketball player. Her skin felt like the finest velvet and I stroked it gently. I kissed her sweet cupid bow mouth that, if she could smile, would show her deep dimples, and I started to sing to her like I've done with all my babies. First *Hush Little Baby*, then *Jesus Loves Me*. I added *Rock a Bye Baby,* but used the version I grew up with, not the traditional lyrics:

> *Rock a bye baby*
>
> *Going night-night*
>
> *You are your mommy and daddy's delight*
>
> *It doesn't matter whatever you do*
>
> *You know that your mommy and daddy love you.*

In her bassinet was a disposable camera. I think the nurse told me there was still some film in it if I wanted to take some pictures. Because Karis had died in utero, probably two days prior to my delivering her, she had some skin slip. For those who aren't familiar, it's where the first layer of skin peels back and can look redder than normal. Karis had this on her head, her eyelids, on her arms and legs, but her hands were spared. I chose to take pictures of me and her holding hands and of her holding the rosary. I took a photo of my parents with Karis, my mom with tears rolling down her face, my dad brokenhearted. I didn't think to do it, but I wish someone had taken a picture of me holding Karis. So many more pictures. But this was 2007. Honestly, we were all doing the best we could.

Cameron never saw her after delivery. That was my decision. Because of the skin slip, I didn't want her memory of Karis to be something frightening or ugly. Should I have done things differently? I wonder. Probably. But again, grief doesn't give you instructions or an owner's manual.

One thing I did was dismiss the nun at the hospital who, bless her, tried to comfort me. She was kind but somewhat overbearing. I wanted my own pastor. He and his precious wife came as soon as we asked even though he and his family had just joined our church maybe a month prior. That's the thing about Methodist churches, they move pastors around every few years. I only wanted MY pastor. He was a kind, gentle man who had crinkly Santa Claus eyes when he smiled. And his wife was like your best friend, mom, and counselor all wrapped into one. The two were the epitome of service and exuded love, compassion, and peace, which I really needed.

"I want Karis baptized," I told my pastor.

"You know, she's already in heaven, you don't have to do this," he said.

"I want to. I want to show God that I'm dedicating her to Him. It's important to me."

So my sweet, dear pastor looked around my hospital room. He took up a full water bottle and said, "This will work." And right there, he blessed the water and baptized Karis. A little sprinkle on his hand which he laid on her forehead. Yes I knew she was already saved, redeemed, reached salvation, and entered the gates of heaven. I knew that in my heart. Of course God would welcome her. How could he not? Part of me was still perplexed by His decision to let her die. But I wasn't in a frame of mind to argue with Him. I only thought in my head, 'We'll talk soon.'

After we spent some time with Karis, I knew it was time to say goodbye. There wasn't a fancy cooling bassinet we could use, no way to take her home like some families can do today. No local photographer willing to come in and take beautiful shots of our Karis so we'd have actual photographic memories. I knew she'd start to deteriorate soon and I felt the urgency from the nurses that our time was coming to an end. They asked if I wanted her to keep her pink outfit on to go to the funeral home, but I couldn't part with it. I asked that she be put in a simple white tshirt and diaper, I needed the physical garments that had touched her body to take home with me. Does that make me a bad mom? Maybe. Selfish? Maybe. But this was all the tangible proof that she existed that I had.

One thing that happens after you've had a stillbirth is that the hospital wants to move you off the maternity ward. They don't want you to hear the newborn baby cries, mother's moaning during birth, proud daddies and families celebrating in the corridor. So after the epidural wore off, the hospital transferred me to a general floor. I remember it being so quiet. No babies crying. No trace of childbirth happening around me. Just silence, very similar to the delivery room when Karis was born.

An aide came in with a meal for me to eat. I couldn't tell you what it was or what time I received it. I'm not sure I ate. I don't remember. She asked how I was feeling and I told her my daughter was stillborn. Yeah, I just blurted it out. I didn't know the protocol yet for talking to people about what happened to Karis.

"Oh honey, you'll have another baby. I see it all the time."

Part of me was angry. Karis wasn't some puppy you could replace with another! I chalked up her careless response to ignorance and tried to give her grace. But maybe she knew something I didn't at the time. Maybe that comment started a new conversation about our future. Maybe it just lingered in my mind as a 'what if.'

But now wasn't the time to consider anything like that. My baby was in the morgue at the hospital and I was in some generic hospital room far removed from all the other new mamas and their babies. It was like I was quarantined so I wouldn't infect others with a tragedy that nobody wants to imagine or live through.

The next morning as we packed up our things, I heard a soft knock at the door. A lovely older couple from my church had stopped by to check on me. The husband was a former pastor and he spoke in soft tones. His lovely wife handed over a single red rose from their garden, the fragrance permeating the room and erasing the sterile hospital smell. I remember her handing me the rose and I immediately felt one of the petals. It felt just as soft and velvety as Karis's skin. I wanted to hold that petal and stroke it forever.

I held that rose and the few things that were Karis's and we got in the car. "I want a cigarette. I want to feel bad and terrible inside and outside. Don't tell me no. Don't talk me out of it." I hadn't smoked in more than a year, definitely not when I was pregnant. But at that point in time, I didn't care. I dared life to challenge my decision. I couldn't care less what life wanted from me. I wasn't suicidal, but honestly, if I happened to die, I wouldn't have been mad about it. I just wanted to be with Karis. I know that sounds self-serving and selfish especially with a family at home who loved me. I was just hurting. I wanted to close my eyes and then open them to see my baby. Alive, whole, and healthy… I'm pretty sure I'd have given up my life for that.

Let me sing the praises of my small town local funeral home. I know, weird to bring this up, right? But funeral homes don't bother me. I'd grown up around them all my life. Death isn't scary. It's part of life. My Nana, my maternal grandmother, worked at a funeral home where she 'make up the ladies' who had passed. She'd do their hair, makeup, nails and dress them so they'd be pretty. When I was growing up, just a kid, I went many times just to help and my Nana would tell me sad stories that sometimes people didn't have visitors after they passed. She'd take extra care to make sure these ladies were just perfect. Even if we were the only two who would see them.

Anyway, after the nurse took Karis away, our instructions were to contact our local funeral home. At this funeral home was a woman who had just started working there to help families through the funerary process. Everyone needs a bit of hand-holding during this, and this sweet lady was good at what she did. Did I mention she also worked for my church in their nursery and their day school? Everyone who had babies at our church knew Na-Na. And Na-Na helped raise our babies. So when the hospital called for pickup and said who and what it was for, my sweet Karis got a personal transport with Na-Na at the helm. Na-Na brought her in, she made me hand-prints in plaster and ink hand-prints on pink cardstock. And at night, she tucked Karis in.

We opted to have Karis cremated (and the funeral home provided a white casket). Na-Na was right there with her through it all making sure she was well taken care of. And let me tell you something else, that funeral home didn't charge us a dime. I will forever be grateful for all of their kindness. They are good people in my eyes. Anyone who will seek to comfort over seeking to gain…those are special people.

Honestly, I really didn't want a memorial service. I was so deep with my grief, I just wanted to go home with it and wallow. Or 'waller.' The term is interchangeable depending on where you live. We Southern Ladies know what wallerin' is. You just slowly settle yourself in the muckity muck and let it overtake you bit by bit. It's stinky and messy, wallowing. I don't think anyone has a vision of wallowing as something clean and bright. It's nasty and dirty. So I was set on "wallerin'".

But then a sweet Samaritan called me. She was a former neighbor of one of my bible study friends and she wanted to reach out to me. I listened and heard her name, Jennifer, and stopped. I might have gasped. I was speaking with an old friend who I had known since second grade! I had no idea she had moved to the area I was in. I also didn't know she had a stillborn son she had lost. What this incredible woman did with her grief was to create a Children's Park that memorialized and honored children who had passed and allowed their families to come and celebrate their life in a number of ways.

I received this phone call and heard this voice from my past – she might have still held a slight English accent from when I first met her in second grade, I don't know. But what I do know is that she offered to come to Karis's memorial. And she offered to make a video for me.

"This may not be something you want to view now. It might be a year or years from now or never. But I want you to have that opportunity when you're ready to see this. Your memorial day will be hard. You'll be overwhelmed by the outpouring of love and grief from your friends, family, church, and community. This will give you time to see Karis's memorial in your time when and if you're ready. And I want to do that for you."

I called the funeral home. I called the church. I coordinated a date and time that would be available between the two. Sunday, November 11, 2007, after worship services. The exact time and day of my scheduled baby shower. Friends and staff mentioned food had already been prepared for the shower. It would be a shame to waste it. We planned the service to be held in the sanctuary with a reception to follow at my parents house 45 minutes away. I just knew it was a safe place to be. So that's what we did.

I Held an Angel Today

I held an angel today.

There were no angel's wings, only small delicate hands

That held a string of beads, intertwined among long slender fingers.

There was no long flowing gown of white,

Only one of delicately knit pink swaddling, all that separated her from my arms.

There was no halo of gold…that I could see anyway…

But, a delicately knit pink cap lovingly made by those whose job they've taken to clothe angels

I held an angel today.

How do I know so much about angels?

Well, I introduced myself to one a half-decade ago, and I still hold her every chance I get.

I'm Papa to only a few angels, so I get to make up the rules.

You know, when a Papa needs to hold an angel, he gets to do what he wants.

My little angels know that.

Sometimes, they kid me and play hard to get, but Papa knows.

I held several angels today; yes, tears were for sorrow, but lots were for joy too.

I held an angel today.

As I stood and gently rocked her in my arms

She quietly slept as if to say, Papa and Gootie, I'm OK.

As if to say, you'll be OK too…and Mommy and Daddy and big sister and all your other angels.

It's only fitting that her name signifies "grace",

Because it's with grace that she brought so many together in her short time.

So, don't ever doubt; angels are not unaware.

How do I know this? Well…I held an angel today.

That was the poem my Daddy, the girls' Papa, wrote about Karis. He asked if he could share it at her memorial but first he needed to read it to me so we could get our crying out. The plan was that during the memorial he could look to me, and I promised to be composed enough so he could read it without breaking down. I remember us being in his garage. The ceiling was very high so his voice echoed. My Daddy's voice has always had a gentle cadence to it, deep and comforting. I sat on a bar stool, him standing about eight feet away, just the two of us girding our grief with a little distance between. I listened to every word, felt every emotion. We cried, sure we cried. But by Karis's memorial day, Daddy had the strength to read it aloud and I held him with my eyes and projected as much love to him as I could as he stood at the pulpit at church.

My sweet mama tried to hush her noisy family before we processioned into the sanctuary. The church speakers played Bruddah Iz's version of *Over the Rainbow*. The song still brings me comfort. I didn't hear it on the radio often, but when I did, or it was featured in a movie even years later, I would always think of my girl from that day on.

My goodness, that church sanctuary was filled to standing room only. I had printed a single photo from that yellow disposable camera that I felt I could share and had it displayed at the altar. The rest of the images, the ones that showed Karis's face, were marred by the skin slip she had and I didn't want to share those upsetting images. Looking back, maybe it would have been ok. I just didn't want people to be repulsed or offended, which is silly now that I think about it. To me she was perfect. What's more repulsive or offensive to us as a species than the death of a child? The only photos that didn't show her skin slip were two that showed me holding her hand in mine, and that tiny pearl rosary. That's the one I chose to share at the memorial.

I remember my precious pastor, the same one who baptized her, giving her eulogy. At one point the sound person was trying to cue up a song a friend had gifted me, but it wouldn't play. After a long stretch of silence, the pastor smiled over to me, "I think Karis is playing with the sound equipment." That made me smile too. To think my precious child was there, showing us she was right there with us, that was comforting. I think every person there felt her presence. I certainly felt their love and fervent prayers over me and my family. A dear friend who lived across the street from the church offered to let Cameron come over and jump on their trampoline if the service was too overwhelming. You have to remember, she was only five. I let her go. Then this same friend shared with me, "I lost a baby too." This wouldn't be the last time I heard those words from people around me. United in a club no one wanted to belong to.

A few evenings after the memorial, we were riding in my folks car heading home. The sun was setting and I happened to look out the window. A vibrant pink sky had developed like an old Polaroid picture, slowly becoming more distinct and vibrant. And across the sky as far as you could see were two airplane contrails that made a perfect cross in the sky. Turning to Cameron, I pointed out the window and exclaimed, "Look, Baby! See that? That's how much God loves you." To which she responded, "God must have let Karis paint the sky. It's our favorite color." I held onto that. I needed something to hold onto. My faith was tried through the loss of Karis, but I still believed in God and that with Him, I could get through this journey.

This was my sign from Karis, I believed. I just felt it in my heart. Whenever I saw a pink sky, I could feel her close. I loved thinking God let her have this gigantic paintbrush and wash the sky in pink.

I don't know if you are aware but after a loss like this, I did like many others do. Hunt for ways to memorialize your child. I signed up for candles to be lit in a cathedral in France, mass was said for Karis in a church in New York. I loved being able to see her name in print as something tangible that said, "Karis was here."

In one of my searches, I came across this beautiful soul in Perth, Australia who was offering to write your child's name in the sand on a beautiful white sand beach near her home. It was a special place where she connected with her son who had been born still a year before. It was all done freely, without cost. She did it out of the kindness of her heart and to honor her son as well. So I emailed her Karis's name. There was a wait of course. Not all days are beautiful and photo worthy. But I remember a couple of weeks later getting a notification that Karis's name in the sand was ready. I scrolled through countless photos trying to find hers, noting every picture I passed, there was a family somewhere in the world who was hurting and hoping to heal just a little because of this gift.

On the day that my photo for Karis was taken (all the photos in our group were taken on the same day) I noted it was a bit overcast. One stood out. I sat at my computer, stunned. Here was Karis's name, written in the sand. Above, it was a pink sky. The light had broken through just long enough for her photograph, the only one with a pink sky. You could see how the sky changed as names changed making each unique. But mine was more than a kind stranger's gift. It was the beginning of healing and an answered prayer. Halfway around the world, in a moment captured, was my pink sky. For my girl, for my Karis.

But even after the hugs, the offering of condolences, beautiful memorials, visits from friends both nearby and from my past, the flurry of activities that numbs you to your new reality fades away. People go back to their everyday lives. The world continues to turn. The sun rises and sets. And now I was angry. How could anyone POSSIBLY go about their day, breathing in and out like it's easy to do, laugh out loud, argue with their spouse? How could the birds dare to sing or the stars glitter? Didn't they know?! My child was gone. She's dead. Please life, just pause. Stop. I can't do this. But life had another blow to deal me.

Numbness leaves. Enter grief.

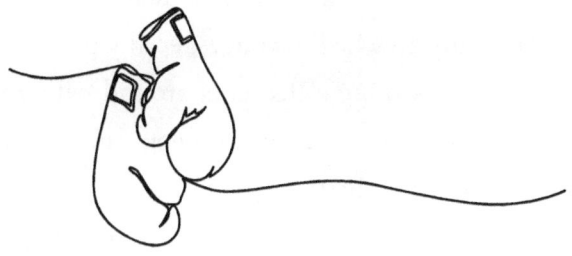

Grace: in the Garage

Hello, Grief. Come on in.

Grief to me is like bringing home a stranger, but without any instructions on how to care for them. Granted, nobody can really prepare you for bringing home a child after birth and what to anticipate throughout babyhood until you actually walk around in the experience and live through it yourself. I get that. When you're anticipating a baby, you read all the articles and books that describe what it's like, what provisions you need, how to prepare, milestones to look forward to. You buy new clothes for you both because you are both growing in positive and beautiful ways. And when it's time, you bring home this beautiful soul that you watch learn and grow and become, while you learn and grow and become a parent. When you lose a child born still, your dreams are shattered. You are shattered. And you have this complete stranger called "Grief" you take home.

With grief, like a newborn, there's a lot of screaming and crying involved. There are endless sleep deprived nights. You don't know who you are anymore. You have no idea where you end, and grief begins. It's constantly attached to you, especially in the early stages of grief. You carry this thing called grief around with you and it's unable to tell you what it needs in ways you can comprehend let alone make sense of. It's a battle between the two of you trying to get to know one another. You try desperately to anticipate what it wants from you so you can just have a little relief from it.

Babies are inherently greedy and want all of you all the time. Grief is the same. There are times you want to run away, scream, bargain with it. "Please, just let me rest just a little bit. Let me get stronger first so I can best handle you. Let me ask the experts and friends and clergy and family to help out first. Can't I put you down for just a moment? Please?"

But part of you – the part still connected to the child you've lost and the grief is all that you have left to hold onto right now. It's tangible. You can feel it in your aching arms. You can taste the metallic taste of the medications they say will help you sleep or function. Your body is still trying to heal from that level-three tear that happened at childbirth and every time you go to the bathroom, there are signs that your baby was born. But you didn't bring home a baby. You only brought home your grief.

This grief wants only you right now. Even when you're still healing from delivery. Even when your breasts are sore because – fun fact! – you still lactate after you've given birth to a stillborn baby. So you carry this close to your heart where cold cabbage leaves are tucked into a tight sports bra and you just want to stop the crying.

I love God, but I was so incredibly angry at God. This is what I get? What have I done that is so bad, so awful to the world that

You thought I deserved for my daughter to die. Especially inside of me, possibly because of something that lived in my DNA that You made in me.

One of the kindest gifts I received after losing Karis was a punching bag. "Here, take the gloves, put them on. You go over to that punching bag and you hit it and punch it and kick it and yell at God and scream and do whatever you need to do to get this out."

So, there, in my messy garage, in my leopard print robe and my sports bra lined with cold cabbage leaves, I let God have it.

"WHY." Punch. "DID. SHE. HAVE. TO." Punch. "DIE? WHAT. DID. I." Punch. "DO. THAT. WAS. SO. WRONG?" Punch. "I. HATE. YOU! I. WANT." Punch. "MY. BABY. BACK!"

Punch. Kick. Scream. Cry. I worked on the bag until sweat dripped from my bra, my hands stinging and aching from the blows I had delivered. Panting, with tears still streaming down my cheeks, I had lost all strength. "I just want her back, God. I hurt so bad. I need You right now."

Don't let anyone say God's not big enough to handle your words or your pain or that He has His reasons for the wrong in the world. All I know is that in my mind, in a whisper I heard, "I'm crying too."

One month after we lost Karis, Bobby came into our life. Full name, Robert Handsome, Bobby was a skinny stray tuxedo cat named after a character my daughter had seen in her favorite TV show *The Naked Brothers Band*. We already had a Maine Coon cat, Hannah who I had nearly my entire adult life. We didn't need another cat, or so I thought. Bobby waltzed into our garage like he belonged with us. And what solidified his living arrangement with us turned out to be a gift from Karis.

I was working one night at my computer and Bobby jumped in my lap and stretched to lay on my shoulder. Bobby was a lover. In that moment I felt that he was just about the same size and weight of Karis and I had this tremendous feeling that his hug was sent from her. I couldn't see her, but every part of me could feel her near.

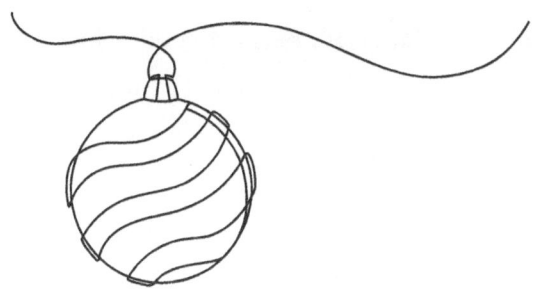

Karis in the Winter: Christmas

It's Christmas time, early morning. Santa has come. Presents have been opened. Stockings, arguably the best present, pilfered and candy eaten. I sit in my quiet living room, the warm glow of white Christmas lights glow and there is a fire in the fireplace. It's a comfortable open floor-plan. Built-in bookshelves flank one solid wall. The colors are coastal but play well with the Christmas colors I've chosen. Lots of vibrant jewel tones, ribbons, Santa Clauses in various colors, and lots and lots of sparkly ornaments. On the tree, on the mantle. Spread around the room. It's a Christmas globe come to life. Stacks of Christmas books on the coffee table. There are smatterings of gold wrapping paper on the floor from the girls opening their presents. Santa *always* wraps his presents in gold wrapping paper. The girls' stockings I've personalized are laying on the floor with various candies, toys, and trinkets spilling out.

My eldest is in her room playing with her latest toys and anticipating me setting up her telescope Santa brought so she can see the stars later tonight. Morgan is down for a nap clearly dreaming of sugarplums and probably the animal of the week she's decided was her favorite. Right now it's just me and Karis.

"Merry Christmas Angel. Have you had a good day?"

"Merry Christmas Mama! It's been so good! I love the new ornament Santa put on the tree just for me. He must love me A LOT!"

I love her childlike wonder.

"Oh, Baby, he loves you so much! Do you want me to read his letter to you again?"

Santa writes to my girls about his adventures and what he has observed throughout the year and when he leaves his presents, he also adorns their individual gifts with matching ornaments. Since Santa (me) "labeled" their gifts with ornaments, he was providing them with their own ornaments for when they were grown and had a home and a Christmas tree of their own.

"Mama, do you ever get sad at Christmas?"

"Why do you ask, Baby? You ok? Come here."

I gather my not-so-little girl in my lap and she rests her head against my shoulder. I absentmindedly stroke her hair in effort to comfort her. She's having big feelings. Holidays can do that to a person regardless of how old or young they are.

I rest my cheek against the top of her head. She instinctively rubs the edge of my robe between her fingers as if to sooth herself.

"Well, sometimes I do. Christmas can be a happy time. But sometimes it makes me sad. You know, my Grandmother Mom, Papa's mommy died on Christmas Day. Cameron was just a little baby. But I have sweet memories of Mom too. She thought Cameron was her baby and she didn't understand how I could be old enough to have a little baby."

Karis giggles. "Christmas just seems kind of like a happy time but sometimes it's sad."

"I know Angel. It's ok to feel what you feel. I'm just glad I've got this time with you right now. That makes me happy."

Karis squirms and hops off my lap and heads to her Big Sis's room.

"I love you, Mama," she says as she disappears around the corner.

"I love you too, my Angel. Merry Christmas."

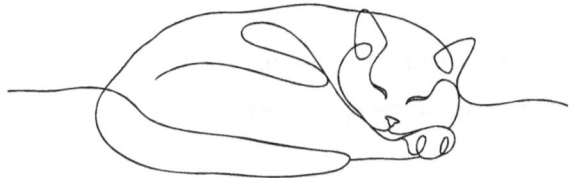

Grace During the New Year

After we lost Karis, we had been invited to our friends' home to celebrate the New Years and spend the night with them. A break from the trauma we had experienced, they felt we needed a break, something to take our minds off things. We needed that time to just let our children play, socialize, let life pause.

My cat Hannah, the most beautiful Maine Coon cat had been my constant companion for 15 years. She was feisty, grumpy, gorgeous and loved only me. She tolerated some. Held disdain for most. She was my girl. But she had health challenges including diabetes that required daily insulin shots for a few years. No problem. But right after losing Karis, she made a sharp decline. She could barely hold her head up to drink. She wouldn't eat. I was numb. Please God, not now...not now. The day after New Years, I just knew. Vet visits traumatized Hannah. She didn't have much time left on earth and I made the decision to let her go as gently as possible. I had absorbent blue pads left over from my recent hospital stay and lay one across my lap and gently laid my first 'good girl' in my arms.

Cameron, only five, and always curious sat on the couch next to me while I stroked Hannah and spoke softly to her.

"Mama, is Hannah dying?" I hate that she knows so much about death. She's been through so much. It's not fair.

"Yes, Baby. This is just part of living. We all die and we go to heaven where there's no sadness, no pain, and we live forever and are happy."

"Will Karis be there in heaven to take care of Hannah? Cameron asks.

"I'm sure she's waiting for her." Hannah's breathing slows. She seems comfortable and calm. I stroke her beautiful fur.

"Mama, I'm going to miss her. I miss Karis. Why does everything have to die? It makes me sad."

"I know, Baby. I'm here and we'll be ok. Hannah will be ok. Karis will take care of her."

"But Karis is just a baby. How can she do that?"

"I just trust her honey. Mama's grandparents are there to help in heaven. It'll be ok."

She's FIVE God. I shouldn't have to explain death. AGAIN. To this precious innocent child. She's going through so much. Please God, let this end.

Hannah died peacefully on my lap with my fingers tangled in her beautiful fur. My dad came over to help me bury her under one of the oak trees in the side yard. Her casket was the box that had held Cameron's Santa gift of a telescope. It was the only thing big enough to hold her. Nothing was big enough to hold my grief.

Karis in the Winter

I had to go to the doctor for my six week post-birth checkup. At the time and after many conversations (maybe some predicated by the aide in the hospital), we had decided that we really felt we were supposed to have two children on earth. So I discussed this with my doctor. Was it possible? Was there anything I needed to do or not do to assure this tragedy wouldn't befall us again? She assured me that other than Karis's umbilical being clotted, which could have been pre- or post-mortem, they really had no answers as to why she died. The doctor, after she realized Karis had passed, went back to her office that day and, with the ultrasound technician, poured over my files, my scans, my test results from our amnio – anything they could scour that would explain why a perfectly healthy baby at 33 weeks gestation would just die.

Thankfully we had great health insurance and the doctor, upon hearing my desire to try for another baby, scheduled me for genetic testing. This involves a lot of vials of blood to which you're awarded a single Band-Aid for your trouble. I didn't think about it at the time. I thought it was just routine. I wasn't familiar with genetic testing, just noted there were a lot of tubes with my blood in them.

Christmas and Karis's due date came and went. We made the holiday as festive and cheerful as we could for Cameron. Cameron, that baby of mine. She didn't know what to think. She quietly grieved and it showed by her pulling her hair out a little at a time so that one side of her beautiful blond hair was shorter than the other. All we could do was love on her. She had only turned five when Karis was born.

My birthday falls three days after Christmas. Feel free to make the Christmas/Birthday gift jokes here. I've never had a problem with my birthday falling between two of the biggest holidays. It's like a small pause between two big events. It's kind of nice. That particular birthday morning, around 7:30am, my phone rang. Even though my Dad and I would regularly have coffee together and he was an early riser, I didn't think he'd call me that early even on my birthday. I answered anyway. The voice on the other line said, "Kristen, this is the doctor's office. We know what happened to Karis."

I heard the voice continue, but I didn't register what she said. "I'm sorry. I don't understand. Can you repeat that please?" Without stopping for a full breath, the voice quickly said "Your genetic test results have come back and confirmed you have a genetic blood clotting disorder called Factor V Leiden. You were born with it and it can cause your blood to clot in certain circumstances. In your case because of your pregnancy and hormones. It's rare and it's not something the doctors or hospitals test for since patient genetic testing is still pretty new. We're just glad we now have an answer we can give you. Your blood clotted in the umbilical and most likely caused Karis's heart to stop."

Lady, I thought, you gotta take a breath.

She went on. "But you've indicated that you want to try to conceive again and we have a plan and medications we'd like to discuss with you."

Pause.

"When could you come in to speak with the doctor?"

That was my birthday present from Karis. "We have an answer. You could try again."

According to my doctor, I would need to agree to start immediately giving myself daily injections of Lovenox, a powerful, yet stable, blood thinner. This would work better than other blood thinners on the market. She wanted me to start before we would attempt to conceive so the medication was already established in my system. There were no other obstacles for us to start trying.

Apparently, I'm a late-blooming 'fertile Myrtle'. I could have had a basketball team full of kids had I started before I had Cameron at 35. At 40 years old, I once again, became pregnant within three months of trying. And as a special gift from Karis, it started snowing the day we found out.

Cue a flurry of doctors visits both with my ob/gyn and my newly assigned oncologist. The oncologist, a beautiful woman with caramel skin greeted me warmly and stated that she would work in tandem with my ob/gyn to assure that my blood was clotting properly and there were no issues. "Patients like you help make what I do a little easier. As you can imagine, not all my patients have happy endings."

These early days of my new pregnancy, I was still grieving Karis deeply. I wanted to make sense of it, to share our story, to connect with other women who had been through what I'd been through. And now I had something additional to add. Factor V Leiden. Was I the only one? Had other mother's experienced loss and subsequent pregnancies that resulted in healthy children after treatment?

Grace in Spring

I found a website that was geared to moms in general. Within that website were groups based on whatever criteria you entered into the search line. I searched for moms of stillborn children. Moms over 40 of stillborn children. Moms diagnosed with Factor V Leiden (FVL). Moms with FVL trying to conceive. One thing I noted was that many of the moms of stillborns who posted weren't necessarily on the FVL pages. I started responding to posts and asking questions. I discovered many of us moms of stillborns were also trying to conceive again. Many got genetic testing. And some had discovered they had FVL. We discussed treatments, blood thinners, worried about those in our on-line community who didn't have an informed doctor who would do genetic testing and would only prescribe baby aspirin to prevent future clots. We shared, cried, commiserated, celebrated when there was something to celebrate, we created deep friendships. It was our little virtual sisterhood. I still have cherished friendships with women I've never met in person to this day, yet I feel a deeper bond with them than some of my own family. I remember their children, both walking this earth and residing in heaven. We say our children's names and remember important days. During my healing through my grief, this was a lifeline and a way to express myself without judgment. It was a blessing that I found these groups and I will forever be grateful for those women whose paths crossed mine.

One of the true blessings of these connections, I was able to tell my and Karis's story to a large group. Many who were struggling and asking why they lost their child. Karis's story encouraged them to ask for genetic testing, to be assertive in their desire to have more children. Treat me. Don't let what happened to my last child happen again.

I was able to share Karis's story when I felt strong enough to return to my favorite women's bible study. They already knew about Karis, but didn't know about FVL. We had many discussions. A few ladies were tested and discovered they too had FVL which led to better treatment with certain conditions. Some of those who tested positive for FVL had daughters who were trying to conceive and our story prompted conversations to have those daughters tested. A few came back positive with FVL and immediately put on a blood thinner regimen.

I have so much pride in my daughter Karis and her story because I know without a doubt, there are people on this earth because we chose to share our story. She and I did that together. Karis Juliana was here. She made a difference. She mattered.

As much as I began to heal from the trauma of losing Karis, my marriage suffered. A 2010 study published in Pediatrics found that couples with a stillbirth had a 40% higher risk of a relationship break-up compared to couples with a live birth. We were trying to work things out but we both grieved differently. The fact that my husband traveled during the week allowed us to have some breathing room before we were reunited on the weekends, but it also meant we were inside of our own heads, dealing with things alone. And I was home with Cameron who was going through her own grief with the loss of Karis, while trying to stay upbeat about yet another baby on the way. Bless her, I have no doubt that she struggled with wanting to love this new baby just as much as she loved Karis but terrified, what if this baby dies too? So, yes, we were all struggling.

We needed to move forward though. I had another amnio. Same doctor. Same twenty minute ultrasound. Counting fingers and toes. Did we want to know the gender? We did. Of course we did. I was sure it was a boy, even though I had kept Karis's nursery intact after she died. I couldn't bear to change it. It was just so perfect for a little girl. There had been discussions within my friend group to pack up the nursery before I returned from the hospital after delivering Karis because it would have been so painful to come home and see that empty room.

"It's a GIRL!" Shock. I think we were in shock. We kind of laughed, what were the odds? And inside, I was relieved. I could keep Karis's room and let her little sister live and grow and thrive there in her memory.

Discovering we were having another daughter both thrilled and threw us off. The marriage was suffering but Cameron seemed happy. The hair pulling continued. I wondered if she could feel the strain of our marriage in addition to the stress of a new baby coming.

We named our soon-to-be rainbow baby Morgan Eliana. Eliana was a mix of her two older sisters middle names Eli(zabeth) from Cameron and (Juli)ana from Karis. That way her sisters would always be with her. When we discovered that "Eliana" had its own meaning it solidified our decision. Eliana is Hebrew for "God answers." Morgan was an answered prayer.

My ob/gyn and her staff took extra special care of me during my pregnancy. Countless sonograms, stress tests, wellness check ups. I saw them so often that they knew me on site and we began this beautiful, easy rapport. By the end of my pregnancy, my ultrasound tech knit me a pair of pink booties and the staff gave me a large gift bag full of baby goodies. My rainbow baby was everyone's baby.

I was getting bigger every month. I felt just fine and relished the time I could see my growing baby and anticipating her arrival. Because of the blood-thinners I was still on (and would continue three months after delivery) it was decided that we needed to schedule an induction rather than allow me to labor naturally. That way I could stop the medication three days before delivery and have a safe epidural and labor. If I started labor without being off the blood thinners, I would have to delivery naturally with no epidural. That didn't sound ideal to me, but the possibility of natural childbirth being a possibility was always in the back of my mind. I prepared as well as I could with meditation and a birthing ball at the ready.

When it came time to schedule the induction, my doctor and I had a conversation.

"What day this last week of October looks good to you?" she asked.

"Hmm, Halloween would be fun!"

"Heck no I'm not letting you have this precious baby on Halloween! My cousin was born on Halloween and he's just weird."

So October the 29th was scheduled and that day was set on my calendar.

Grace in the Summer

When I was about eight months into my pregnancy, signs in my marriage were pointing towards failure. I suggested marriage counseling. He went to the first and the last session. I went to all the rest. I cried. He stared straight ahead stoically. I thought counseling was helping. He thought it was a waste of time. By the time we had our last session, I knew our marriage was over.

For Cameron's sake we kept things quiet between us. Due to his work schedule and being on the road so much, we really didn't need to cross paths. When he came home on weekends, he put his energy into Cameron. New week - Wash, rinse, repeat. That made delivery day of Morgan much easier as well. We weren't fighting like we had been, we had kind of developed an understanding as well as a rhythm for our life. We could be friendly. And we entered the hospital – the same one I had Karis in – more like roommates. Roommates about to become parents again.

Nervous anticipation. Excitement. Fear. Relief that we were almost at the end. We had all the feels going into the delivery room. Again my parents were there. Again my mom put on earrings so she could look pretty for her new granddaughter. Sister girlfriends and church members kept a steady stream of visitors coming through until it was time to push.

The room was silent except for the doctor giving me instructions. We held our breath. One last push and Morgan was earth-side. Deep breath. She gave one cranky cry as she reached out. All I could see from my vantage point was these long graceful fingers. Fingers of a piano player. She was safe, she was here, she was alive. Thank you, God. Thank you Karis.

Even though out marriage was on the outs, we decided to co-habitate at least until Cameron finished Kindergarten. That was the plan. Plans change, of course. We lived together until Morgan was five-weeks-old. We were done and had enough of each other. I was terrified, lost, but I knew I was strong enough to get through this part of my journey.

The girls and I were blessed to live with my parents after my ex-husband and I split up. We sold the house my dad had built us. The one right next door to my brother. It kind of broke my heart, but as a newly single mom, I had to do what needed to be done. I sold nearly every possession we had with the exception of essentials and memories that would fit in 10x10 storage space. We stayed with my parents for more than two years while I built up a reserve that would support me and my babies in a town that had embraced us during the worst of our storms.

I do recall this one time before we moved out. Morgan couldn't have been more than two. We were on the back porch of my Mom and Dad's place where they had this 30' screened in porch. It was perched above the trees and above the ground where "critters" came to eat deer corn and hummingbird nectar. Morgan leapt out of her Papa's arms and ran down the porch pointing at the tree tops, "Karis! Karis! Hi, Karis! Hi!" she exclaimed. This baby didn't know the name Karis or the meaning. But she pointed to the trees and it's like she just knew. Her sister was there playing among the leaves and let her little sister know she was there. Angels among us.

Thoughts: Outliving Our Children

It's been said outliving your children is unnatural. An abomination. I don't dispute this. It is a perverse twist of life that no parent should have to face or bear. There's not even a name for bereaved parents like 'widow' or 'orphan' that explains your loss. *Viloma* is about as close as it gets, meaning 'against the natural order.'

But after 18 years of life without Karis, maybe today I feel different. There may not be a name, but maybe there's a feeling I can pinpoint and say, 'yes, that's me.' Maybe today I can say 'I provided my child heaven on earth.' Karis knew only gentleness, safety, nourishment, peace. There was no pain, no cold, no suffering. We danced together in the living room and rocked under warm showers. I know my child heard me sing and tell stories to her big sister and laugh. I prayed aloud. Delighted in life's passage with hands on my belly gently stroking. Do I wish my child was born breathing and fighting for life? Yes.

But am I grateful that all she knew was Love?

Also, yes.

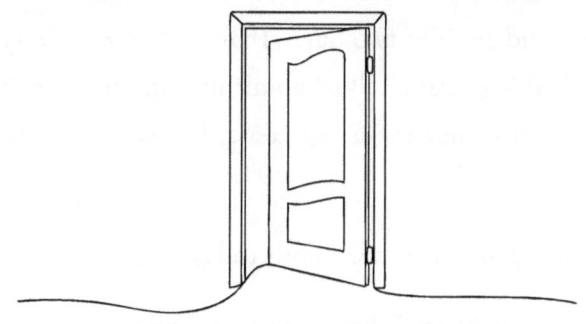

My Randy: Boundaries

I'm showing My Randy a few images I saved as my Lock Screen photos on my phone. Each one a visual reminder of what we worked on each week. Step out on faith like Indiana Jones in *The Raiders of the Lost Ark* bridge scene. Click!

Describe to me what a boundary looks like to you. I visualize a clear, flexible fence surrounding green grass and blue skies above. Safe. Click!

I'm creating a gallery in my mind and on my phone of images that prompt me into new ways of thinking every time I wake up my screen.

"You're obviously a visual person, especially with your line of work. These are good." He hands me back my phone.

I need them right now. I want to be brave. Those images will help me be brave.

"Let's do an exercise," Randy begins. "Close your eyes."

After my sessions with Randy, if he recommended a book, I order it on Amazon and get it in two days. Thanks, Prime delivery. They're in line with things we've talked about during our time. Some are books he has his students in class read. I look at these books like lifelines.

"What would you like to talk about today."

I smile. "I read Eckhart Tolle's book you recommended. *The Power of Now*. Read it in three days."

My Randy's eyes widen. "Really? Three days? Did you not notice throughout the book it says 'pause' so you can just sit in what you've just read? My students usually get at least half a semester to read that book. It can be intense."

"It was like drinking from a fire hydrant. 'Being present. Finding peace. Acknowledging time is fluid.' Mind freeing stuff," I say.

I hesitate. "Actually, I want to talk about Karis today. It's time. I need to talk about her. I'm beginning to forget things."

Randy looks up. "We can talk about anything you want. This is your time."

"We only have 55 minutes, Randy. I could talk about her and our story for hours." I reach for the pillow on the couch. I'm feeling vulnerable and my body feels exposed.

"Why don't you talk *to* Karis instead?" he asks.

"I talk to her all the time. When I see pink skies, when I see her picture or urn on my dresser, lots of times."

"Yes, but do you *see and hear* her when you talk to her?"

I look towards the ceiling, grasping the pillow over my midsection. "I mean, I imagine what age she might be, maybe what attributes she and her sisters might share. Or share with me. But nothing solid, nothing detailed." I break my heart a little. It seems obvious that I should envision what my daughter would look like, sound like, BE like. Part of me feels like I've done her a disservice in how I've kept her memory alive. Always in abstract. Never something solid, tangible. Nothing I could hold.

Randy clarifies, "I can tell you have a very vivid imagination just by the pictures you save on your Lock Screen. What if you created a special place in your mind that was safe and peaceful. Someplace you could visit Karis anytime you wanted, for as long as you wanted, do you think that would be helpful?"

"You think it'll make a difference." A statement. Not a question.

"I do," Randy nods. "Imagining a loved one in a mentally created place can be helpful because it uses the brain's ability to change through neuroplasticity and can create positive feelings, but it's most beneficial when it's a healthy coping mechanism, not an avoidance behavior. The brain processes imagined experiences similarly to real ones, activating mirror neurons and strengthening neural pathways associated with the thought, which can help shift perspective and provide comfort."

"What book did you get that out of?" I half grin.

He returns the smile, "Read it on the Internet."

I raise my eyebrows. "That's actually an interesting idea. I'm willing to give it a shot."

Randy settles back in his chair.

"Close your eyes. Imagine a place that is safe and peaceful. Special. It'll always be there if you want to visit Karis. It's a place you two can come anytime you want to be together or talk. No one can take that place away from you. Now, tell me, what do you see, smell, hear, feel."

In my mind, I open my eyes.

I open a door to a cabin. My cabin. One that, in my imagination, I would have built years ago…

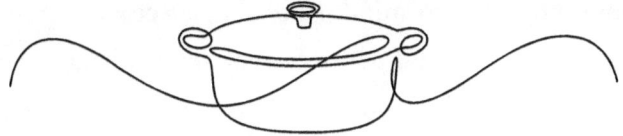

Karis in the Fall

I imagine myself at our cabin again. My and Karis's cabin. And I reflect on the number of places and conversions I've created in order to keep my daughter's memory alive. Today, I just want my baby.

I walk in the door. Inside, it smells of warm vanilla. My Nana, my mother's Mama greets me. I have missed her so much. Seeing her auburn hair and cornflower blue eyes behind her wire rimmed glasses hitches my breath.

"Hi, Baby! You hungry? I've got potato salad in the fridge. There's beans and cornbread." Nana pauses, "Want a little ham?" This is a family joke which makes me laugh, and I gather my sweet five foot tall grandmother in my arms and hug her tight.

"How's my girl, she good for you today?" I ask.

"Oh honey, she's just fine. Down for a nap. Why don't you sit down a minute and tell me how you're doing?"

"I'm doing pretty good. I'm sure you've heard all that's gone on. But I'm doing ok. Taking things day by day."

Nana reaches over and pats my hand and smiles at me across the breakfast table. Somehow my grandmother's dining nook is now part of my cabin. I don't mind. I note Nana's crooked pointer finger, the same finger she'd dip into cake batter or whatever Southern delicacy she was making and let us have a taste. I have a crooked Nana finger I notice.

"You know we're always here for you, Baby."

I love how she still calls me "Baby".

I hear in the back bedroom that Karis has started to stir. Smiling, Nana takes off her apron, the one my Nanny sewed and my own Mama gifted to me. Flour sack floral with red trim. She hangs it on the pantry door. "I'm gonna get back to your Pampaw and let you settle in with Karis. Oh, I left you a pound cake on the counter and made Nanny's cake sauce. I think it's still warm. I love you."

"I love you, too. Give Pampaw sugars for me and tell him I love him."

"I will," Nana says as she kisses me goodbye. "See you soon, Baby."

I walk back into a nursery that is fit for any 'girly' girl. Sage green walls. Roses and antiques and tchotchkes. Pink patchwork and wire butterflies on the wall. Over the window a banner in with ballet pink letters that spell ANGEL. I move quietly to the white crib in the corner and look down in wonder at this beautiful baby girl I've created. She's awake, but not fussy. Her blue eyes burrow into mine and I can't help but stroke her brow and coo at her. I gently lift her being careful to support her head and bring her to my chest and lay her head against my heart. Warmth floods over me. I feel the rise and fall of her breaths – in and out. I bend down to inhale her scent. Something like petrichor and tropical flowers that grow wild. She smiles and coos with a toothless grin. My baby, my Karis.

Mama's home.

And I dance her into the living room, our time together never-ending, humming "Into the Mystic."

THE END FOR NOW

Thank you for following me through this journey. I hope it has brought you comfort, peace, and understanding.

So much of my healing has taken place purely in my thoughts, remembering, and trying to make it as vivid as possible so I can supplant new memories. I'd like to give you a little gift to you, Dear Reader, my Nanny's cake sauce recipe.

My Nanny (Vesta Benjamin White Luttrell) was my Nana's (Frances Elizabeth White Davis)'s Mama. My Nanny cared for me when I was just a baby while my very young parents worked. She carried me like a football because she required the use of a cane to walk. I still can recall the creak of her floors in her turn of the century house and the smell of her kitchen. Always something sweet in the air. Nanny would have a pound cake, homemade of course, available for company as any good Southern lady would. In addition, she would make a warm cake sauce to pour on top of cake slices, served in fancy depression glass dishes. I recently asked my Mama about it, "do you remember?"

Not only did she remember, she had the recipe. 'Cake Sauce' isn't a custard nor is it an icing. It's almost like cake 'gravy.' Stay with me here, particularly if you're like me and have to hand in your Southern Card because 'you're just not a fan of 'wet bread'.' (Biscuits and gravy aren't my favorite - but that's a story for another day.) 'Cake Sauce' is something sweet, simple, and when my Mama resurrected the recipe just this year, awoke serious memories in my soul. It's comfort and love and family. So my gift to you is this. Make it. Serve it with a simple unfrosted cake or pound cake. Preferably still warm from the oven. The sauce is served warm as well and you eat it with a spoon so you get every last drop. I hope you enjoy.

Nanny's Cake Sauce

On medium heat, melt one stick of real salted butter in a sauce pan.

Stir in one heaping soup spoon (the bigger of your silverware spoons) of flour. Add one cup white sugar. Cook together for about one minute to make a sweet roux.

Slowly add 2 cups, plus 1 teaspoon, milk (we use whole milk). Cook with a whisk until thickened. Add one teaspoon of vanilla extract at the end and stir.

Serve sauce warm over a slice of cake in a pretty dish. Eat with a spoon.

Note from my Mama: *If I were you I'd make a double batch. I had to make another batch before the pound cake was gone!*

Love you!

Acknowledgments

I would like to take this time to thank a few people without whom I would not have been able to be here in order for this book to become a reality.

To my girls, Cameron and Morgan. Cameron my miracle child, our Big Sis, and Morgan my rainbow baby, lovingly called Little Miss. How I love you. Thank you for keeping your sister's memory alive and for loving me, faults and all.

To my parents, Ron and Sue Merritt. No better parents or grandparents could be asked for. You are by far the best Gootie and Papa that my girls could have. I love you beyond measure. Thank you for your constant and loving support throughout this journey.

To my husband, Jon Gowen. You are my person, my sweet man. Thank you for believing in me and encouraging me to write this story. Karis is just as much yours as she is mine. I love you.

To My Randy. Yes, I know your full name now, and I discovered we have mutual friends who have offered your contact info. But don't worry! Out of an abundance of respect, I will continue to honor your boundaries and not seek you out. But I hope somehow you know I appreciate all you have poured into this lady who was so broken. She can now deal with whatever life throws her way. This story would have not happened without you providing me with tools and guidance during the year we met together. I am so grateful.

To my countless family and friends who have lifted me up during the unimaginable and continuing to remember our Karis, thank you from the bottom of my heart. Keep sending me photos of pink skies, writing her name in the sand, and saying her name aloud.

To my former church, First UMC Lindale, my WinGS sister/girlfriends, Shelley and Na-Na in the nursery, and all my church family. You showed up and became the hands and feet of Jesus that I and my family needed. I will never forget you for that. I know many of us have drifted apart or have new roles in life (I'm looking at all you Grandmothers now!) Please know I will forever hold that time we had as sacred and I love you for loving me, my family, and Karis. Thank you. Now, go let your babies play in Karis's playground because that's where angels and friends meet.

And a special note to those whose lives have been irreversibly changed by the loss of a child, know I see you. I will say your children's names. I will never forget.

Karis Soundtrack

This is the playlist I was listening to while I wrote this book if you would like to take a listen. If I may be so bold as to suggest, listen to these love songs from the perspective of a mother to her child. That's what I did.

Scan the QR Code

https://music.apple.com/us/playlist/karis/pl.u-vxy6k04CzqA-BL2x

www.ingramcontent.com/pod-product-compliance
Lightning Source LLC
Chambersburg PA
CBHW020948090426
42736CB00010B/1316